How We Create Our Suffering And What To Do About it

A Whole New Way to Think About Mental Health

Ravinder Gino Hoonjan

Dedication

I dedicate this book to my family - Dad Harpal (Billa), Mum Ranjit (Rani), my Gran and Grandad, my brothers Gurmit (Bookie), Daljit (Mina), Sandeep (Sam) and my sister Simran (Sim), and the legends that were, Sheppie the 1st, 2nd, and the current 3rd, as well as our new addition, Rolo, who without all their love and support, I would not be here writing this. I love you all dearly!

All my dear friends have supported me with everything I've wanted to do and encouraged me to pursue my dreams. You know who you are. I love you all.

This book (especially my story) may shock most, as I've never really shared this. I do this in an attempt to help and inspire all those who are suffering needlessly. If I make a difference to just one person, I feel this vulnerability will be worth it.

DISCLAIMER: This book is for informational purposes only and does not substitute for professional help. If you suffer from mental health illness, always consult your doctor or mental health practitioner before starting something new or changing anything.

ISBN: 9798644788439

Imprint: Independently published

Contents   Page

'The journey of a thousand miles begins with a single step.'

Lao-Tzu

Impact Of The Three Principles

What you are about to learn is entirely different from most books in the self-help section. The three principles have been growing in popularity for many years and have positively impacted many people around the globe.

Many people have returned from severe mental illnesses such as psychosis and schizophrenia to perfect mental health.

Countless people have recovered from severe anxiety and panic attacks to calmness and well-being.

Severe drug and alcohol addictions have been broken by many to a life of sobriety and health.

Thousands of people have broken free from fears and negative beliefs to live fuller, richer lives without the shackles that held them back.

This understanding has transformed Rundown, Drug, and crime-ridden communities into peaceful, friendly areas to live in.

Many have found a new love and zest for life with a

sense of inner calm and well-being. They have discovered the true meaning of freedom and health.

Many psychologists and psychiatrists have incorporated the three principles into their work with clients, often producing 'miraculous' results that defy conventional psychology.

After incorporating this understanding into their workplace, many businesses have seen a dramatic profit increase and reduced sickness and attrition rates. Workplace culture improved, as well as team and interdepartmental synergy.

Many have been relieved from suffering chronic physical pain after relieving the chronic mental stresses they endured.

The list goes on and on, but needless to say, the three principles have had an enormous impact. Mental health and well-being are within every single person on the planet, including you. Armed with this new understanding, you can finally move from mental illness and stress to mental health and well-being.

'You don't find a diamond lying on the surface; it is buried deep in the ground. You need to uncover it.'

Me

Introduction

Why I Wrote This Book

I've wanted to write a book for as long as I can remember. Over the years, I've made many attempts to create a book worth reading. I would start but would run out of ideas and steam. My hard drive has at least half a dozen uncompleted books, which will probably never get completed. So, what is different this time around?

As I type these words, we are in the middle of the lockdown of the Coronavirus pandemic. People are suffering. Anxiety, depression, and suicidal ideation are on the increase. The world needs connection; people need support. Isolation is driving many people crazy. Mental health issues are rising, and we must do something about them.

These unusual and challenging times allowed me to slow down from the usual mental rush and noise. One night, lying in bed, I had an 'insight.' An idea popped into my head to share what I have learned over the years about the three principles to help people suffering from mental health issues. I created an online resource portal sharing the three principles and innate health (I will use these terms interchangeably as they refer to the same thing), specifically to help those suffering needlessly. It was to spread the understanding from some of the most brilliant and insightful people in the field, ranging from high-end coaches to psychologists and psychiatrists, who all point to how our minds work and how we experience life. For years, these people tried to help people using their knowledge and expertise with limited success.

It is interesting to note that these highly educated people with degrees in psychology or psychiatry, at some point, suffered from mental health issues such as depression and anxiety themselves. This went on for years until they came across the three principles. As they looked more in the direction of innate health, they noticed how their anxiety and depression lifted, and they started feeling better than they had in years. They shared it with their clients, who were suffering for years and noticed that their clients also began to get better.

Since then, they focused their attention in this direction, and more and more people became involved and began sharing the principles with seemingly miraculous results. I will share more about the birth of the three principles and what they are later in this book, but for now, let's continue.

As I was saying, that insight led to the creation of www.globalmentalhealth.co.uk, which is a website dedicated to addressing and changing mental illness to mental health. It is a resource website filled with videos, my podcast, other podcast links, articles, and much more to share this understanding globally. It went from idea to being up and running online in about five days - that's how passionate I am about this. I kept adding content daily, recording my podcast, and writing a blog. The site content grew quite rapidly and will continue to evolve. The insight also led me to want to share my story, hence this book: my journey, my suffering, my depression, and my anxiety to mental health and well-being. I wanted to show how I went from suffering to understanding how I was creating my suffering to never feeling like that (or that bad) again.

I request that you temporarily suspend your beliefs and read this with an open mind. I don't want you to believe what you read in this book but to use it to look in that direction and see if it rings true for you.

My aim for this book is to inspire you to look in a new direction: to re-evaluate your ideas about mental illness and suffering and to rediscover your innate health and well-being. To realise that you are not broken or in need of fixing. We were innocently misunderstanding where our experience was coming from. You are whole and complete. You just don't know it (yet)!

<u>2023 UPDATE:</u>

As of this year, the Global Mental Health website no longer exists. The project ran for 2 ½ years, and I felt a new direction needed to progress.

This year, Bright Minds Consultants was created to help share this understanding with organisations, aiming to improve mental health within the workplace and help businesses thrive, regardless of global changes.

www.Brightminds.global

'Be thankful for what you have; You'll end up having more. If you concentrate on what you don't have, you will never ever have enough.'

Oprah Winfrey

My Story

In The Beginning

My story begins the day I was born. It was the 12th of April 1980 (birthday cards in the post – just kidding), and I was born with a deformity. My left foot had four toes and was touching my shin. I guess I was in such a rush to get out that I didn't have time to develop correctly.

Growing up throughout my childhood, I regularly visited doctors and hospitals to monitor my development. It transpired that my left leg grew a lot slower than my right leg, and by the time I was twelve years old, there was a whopping seven centimetres difference. Surgery was on the cards.

After the surgery, I remember being in the hospital for about a month or so. I recall the pain vividly I felt in my leg post-surgery and was given copious amounts of painkillers in an attempt to reduce the pain. I remember looking down and seeing this metal contraption (an external fixator) sticking out of my shin. I saw four long pins sticking out of my leg, connected by a long bar. I also had my ankle cut, repositioned, and had an internal pin to hold it in place.

After the pain subsided from the initial operation, it was time to set about the lengthening procedure. The rod connecting the pins had a screw on the side of it with an Allen key head. I was told that I had to turn the screw through two-quarter turns, which moved the pins apart and hence lengthened my leg. I had to do this daily, which forced the pins apart by two millimetres. This was unbearable pain, so after reviewing it, the doctors advised me to do one-quarter turn a day, so lengthening became one millimetre a day until we got to the correct length, where both left and right shins were the same. I believe there was a four-centimetre difference in shins and three centimetres between the femurs (thigh bones).

After this was complete, it was time to be placed into a cast and let the bones grow back and heal. During this entire time, I was on crutches, so when I was back at school, I couldn't get involved in playing sports or doing the things that all the other kids my age were doing. I couldn't go on school trips and had to spend much time at home. I remember feeling upset and down about that a lot. I used to wear trousers with the left leg cut at the knee to allow space for the fixator, so it was always on show. I recall vividly people stopping and staring, pointing, etc. and how this made me very self-conscious.

I used to think.

'Why me?'

'What's wrong with me?'

'Why can't I be like the other kids?'

These kinds of questions would play on my mind pretty much daily. I was becoming increasingly self-conscious, but it didn't affect me so much at this stage in my life. But later, I realised that it was very formative to who I would become.

This process from surgery to lengthening to physio and rehab would take just shy of two years, of which my entire time was on crutches. I remember the relief when it was all over, and I could return to being active and enjoying sports. It was at this point that the doctors dropped a bombshell.

THEY WANTED TO REPEAT THE WHOLE PROCEDURE ON MY THIGH!!!

I point blank told my parents I didn't want to go

through with it, and they relayed my objections to the surgeons. The surgeons advised me that if I did not go ahead with the surgery, then I could potentially suffer back issues later on in life, but that fell on deaf ears, and that was the end of that.

I returned for several more checkups over the year and was eventually discharged.

'If you're always trying to be normal, you will never know how amazing you can be'

Maya Angelou

Back To Normality?

After that was all over, everyday life ensued. I completed school and went on to university to study Osteopathy.

But I never felt right. I never felt like I fit in or belonged. I had feelings of inadequacy and often felt anxious being around other people. This wasn't usually visible externally as I became a people pleaser. If people like me, then I must have some worth, right? I was the joker and amuser. The happy face that everyone saw. At night, when I was alone and had time with my thoughts, I was depressed, but I would not talk about this to anyone. That's a sign of weakness, isn't it? Admitting to faults and feelings? Nah, pass, I would not be doing that; thank you very much.

So, on life went. During school, I found a miracle cure for confidence and self-esteem. All negative thoughts would drop away, and I would feel invincible. I'm sure you have heard of it and used it too. It was alcohol. The numbing effects of alcohol were terrific. I would become super funny (well, that's my opinion, and I'm sticking to it) and at ease around people. With this discovery and underage drinking being the order of the day, I managed to have a decent social life and made many friends. However, I still couldn't shake those feelings of inadequacy when I didn't have alcohol in my system.

Fast forward to university. It was much of the same. With newfound freedom (living away from home), I began drinking a lot to cope with the uncomfortable feelings. During the day and in lectures, I lived with constant low laying anxiety that never really went away until that first drink. This is how I passed the years until the day when I came across something that gave me a ray of hope.

'Be the change you wish to see in the world.'

Mahatma Gandhi

WOW! This Is Awesome!

My flatmates and I were sitting around the TV watching Derren Brown, and I distinctly remember one of my friends saying something like

'He does that NLP stuff.'

And that stuck around in my head. The following day, I was still intrigued by this NLP (Neuro-Linguistic Programming) stuff, so I looked it up on the internet. I set up my brick of a laptop and made a cup of coffee while it connected to the internet (we had dial-up connections back then). I spent most of the day looking into NLP and became obsessed. I read all I could and started buying and devouring book after book. I started applying the techniques, and they helped. I started feeling better about myself more of the time.

That was it. I was sold. I decided to learn NLP formally and went to Paul McKenna Training (the hypnotist of the television) to become certified in NLP and then went on to do Master NLP Practitioner training. I spent thousands and thousands of pounds on learning more and more.

I progressed to getting a diploma in Hypnotherapy

and counselling skills and did CPDs in Emotional Freedom Techniques, Cognitive Behavioural Therapy (CBT), and Hypno-Coaching.

At this point, I had dropped out of university to the joy of my parents and started helping people with issues such as confidence, weight loss, anxiety, addictions, etc. Truth be told, some got better, and some did not.

I was having good days and bad days. Some days, I didn't feel the low-level anxiety; other days, it would flare up and consume me. I would do technique after technique to calm and settle myself; some days, it would work, and others, it wouldn't.

At this point, I came across something called the three principles, which I glanced over but didn't really pay attention to as it seemed too simplistic. I thought to myself that I needed to fix myself. I was 'broken,' and the three principles didn't offer any techniques, so that got left to the wayside. On and on it went.

I worked part-time during all this as I would have quite a few clients some months and not many at other times. I was also seeing clients for massage as my dad was in denial about me dropping out of university and would tell all his customers (dad is a self-employed mechanic) who had back issues to

'Go see my son. He will fix you up.'

I would get a regular supply of clients, so I decided to get an actual massage qualification to work on people legally. I got certified in Swedish massage and a Sports Massage and Remedial Soft Tissue Therapy diploma. I had a part-time job, massage and coaching clients, working on myself to see off the depression and anxiety, but I still felt inadequate. I needed more tools and added meditation and mindfulness to the toolbox.

I was desperate to leave my part-time job and work with clients full-time, so my attention shifted to marketing and 'getting clients,' which led me to Steve Chandler's Advanced Client Systems (ACS). This involved me flying to the United States three times to attend seminars run by Steve. They were terrific. I learned a lot and met some fantastic Coaches. One of them was a gentleman named Ankush Jain. I hit it off with him and learned a lot from him from the get-go. He was (and still is) a three principles coach, and this was my reintroduction to the principles. I hired him to coach me about the three principles and getting clients.

As I listened intently, what he was saying started to make a lot of sense. I wasn't broken. I didn't need fixing. I was whole, apart from when my thoughts navigated me away from mental health to mental suffering.

My thoughts were creating my feelings moment by moment. And the more I saw that, the more I realised the truth. I realised that I had been creating all my suffering this entire time, and all the techniques I was applying were an attempt to fix my thinking! Once I realised that there was nothing to fix, and I was sitting in the middle of mental health, and it was my thinking (more so BELIEVING my thinking), which took me away from health to suffering, well then, that changed everything.

This realisation unfolded over several months and is still going on to this very day. The more I looked in this direction of Mind, Thought, and Consciousness, the more at ease I became, and that constant low-level anxiety began to shift, and I began to feel good about myself.

I have continued to look in this direction ever since. Sometimes, I stray and go back to using techniques but then remind myself of what my feelings are telling me at the moment and what to do. Don't worry if this isn't making any sense now; I will explain the three principles later in this book.

I started sharing this with my clients at the time, and they began to realise this for themselves.

As time passed, I began seeing more and more massage and fewer coaching clients. I guess massage was a more comfortable sale than coaching, so the business grew in that direction. My heart was never in massage; it was always to help people suffering like I was, but as life unfolded, I stuck with the easy sell and massage.

That's my story, and now fast forward to 2020. The year I was going to make it. My goal was to leave my part-time job and build a massage business full-time. I had such high hopes, and the year started well. January was my best month yet regarding income and clients, and I could see it growing. And then it all came to a crashing halt!

The coronavirus pandemic swept the globe, and work suddenly stopped. No more clients, and I was furloughed from my part-time job.

What to do?

I thought I would make the most of the time off and chill, learn, read, and spend time with the family. I started reading more about the principles and watching video after video. I began to get a deeper understanding of it and see more about the truth of it all. I always wanted to do something to help people suffering from mental health issues, but nothing ever came to mind. Then, one night, lying in bed, I had an insight to create a resource website where people suffering can go and watch videos, read articles and blogs, and listen to podcasts. I remember saying to myself it would be:

'The Google for mental health!'

It hit me like a ton of bricks. The very next day, I began looking into it, and within five days,

www.globalmentalhealth.co.uk

was up and running. I started recording my podcasts (something I was terrified of doing before the insight) and writing blogs. It gained traction, and I was letting as many people know about it. I was posting on Facebook, Instagram, and WhatsApp statuses. Then, it occurred to me to write a book on suffering, and this is where I am today.

This is why you are reading this book today. Now, let us move on, get to the meat of the book, and talk about suffering and how we create it for ourselves.

Time to Explore

Have a break and do some research for yourself.

Spend some time looking into the three principles and start exploring.

Watch videos and listen to podcasts. You might see or hear a different perspective. You can also listen to my new podcast:

Bright Minds on Spotify

*'Thought creates the world and then says,
I didn't do it.'*

David Bohm

What Are The Three Principles?

Let us first begin by looking at what a principle is. The definition, as found online, is:

'A fundamental truth or proposition that serves as the foundation for a system of belief or behaviour or for a chain of reasoning.'

So, a principle is something that holds true no matter what. For example, the principle of gravity always works, whether you believe it or not. You drop something, and it will hit the ground. In art, the three primary colours make up every other colour in the spectrum. A principle, then, is constant and always holds true.

Let's take a look at flying a plane. Flying a plane is complicated. There are many instruments to watch and things to know for a pilot to fly. They go through years of training to become proficient at it. The engineers who design the planes keep adding more and more tools, equipment, and technology to make them safer and easier to fly. However, for the aircraft to fly, the engineers only need to know the four principles of flight - Lift, Gravity, Thrust, and drag.

Those four principles are what allow the plane to fly.

All engineers know this, which is the foundation they work from to develop planes. They can create the most complicated systems and advanced technology to make the aircraft super-fast and efficient, but if they ignore the principles and the foundations of flight, that plane isn't going anywhere. This leads me to the three principles of human experience.

The three principles were first articulated by a Scottish welder by the name of Sydney Banks back in the early 1970s. He had an enlightening experience through which he talked about the three principles of the human experience. He named them:

Mind

Thought

Consciousness

What do they mean?

Mind – Is the universal energy or intelligence behind life. It is the energy that gives us life. Simply put – we are alive.

Thought – Is the vehicle through which we experience life in our own unique way. Simply put, we are thinkers and not the contents of thought. It's not what we think; it's the fact that we think.

Consciousness – refers to awareness. We have the capacity to be aware of life. It's not what we are aware of; it's that we are aware.

Simplified further,

We are alive

We think

We are aware

These are the principles that Mr Banks spoke about, which are the principles behind all human experience and allow us to be aware of it. They work together all the time, whether we believe them or not. These principles are what enable us to experience life in our own unique way.

This also points us in the direction that life only works one way, from the inside out.

The principles point to how we create our experience from moment to moment. Modern psychology and techniques are typically used AFTER we have had the experience. The methodologies and techniques such as NLP and CBT are all designed to work on thoughts AFTER you have them. You have the thought and experience, and then you apply a technique in an attempt to change that experience. This requires a lot of work, time, and energy. With that being said, it doesn't always work, either.

With the principles, we see HOW we create our experiences and feelings. Knowing that we are the creators of our thoughts, feelings, and experiences allows us a certain sense of freedom from the external world.

What I mean by this is that the more we recognise that the world outside of us CAN NOT make us feel anything WITHOUT us first having thoughts or thinking about it, shows us that we can't be victims of our circumstances unless we choose to be.

At first, we didn't know any of this. Our awareness of how we operate was nonexistent, so it looked like the world was causing us to feel and behave in a certain way. But as we learned more about what Sydney Banks pointed out, we became more aware of how we operate. This puts all responsibility back on us, that we can only feel a certain way about circumstances via our thoughts.

We are solely responsible for how we feel from moment to moment.

Time to Reflect

Pause here and reflect on what you have read.

Does it make sense?

Do you agree with it?

Are you willing to keep an open mind and continue to explore?

Make a mental or physical note of the answers. At the end of the book, I invite you to look back and see if anything changed for you.

'The best way to make your dreams come true is to wake up.'

Paul Valery

It Only Works One Way

On the face of it, it looks like to many (including myself at one point) that life is happening to us. That life happens, and we respond to it accordingly. It can also look like our feelings are brought about by the circumstances that occur in our lives on a day-to-day basis.

Life is hard

Life is tough

People are rude and narcissistic

My life sucks

These are some of the phrases we hear daily (obviously, on the flip side, there are positive phrases too, but in keeping to the book's theme, I will stick with the not-so-positive), and on the surface, it can appear to be true. But ask yourself, how do you know life sucks? Or is difficult? How do you know people are rude?

For you to see life this way, you must have an internal representation of how life should be. Right?

Stay with me here.

Life is neutral in that life happens regardless of how we want it to go. All meaning about life is assigned by you, inside your mind using thought!

Everything you see, perceive, like, and hate is constructed by your thinking. Now, another thing to remember is that:

Your feelings are linked to your thinking and not your circumstances!

Read that again. Your feelings do not come from what's happening in your life. They come from what you THINK is happening in your life.

It's an inside game. We experience life from the inside out, not the other way around.

The process happens instantly and gives the illusion that life is causing us to feel a certain way. Don't believe me?

Good, it would be best if you didn't take my word for it. I invite you to have a look at this for yourself.

Think back to a time when someone really annoyed you. Where their behaviour or words irritated you. Now, if you can try and imagine what was going on in your head at the time. Were you thinking:

'This guy/girl is f***king annoying.'

'Shut the f***k up.'

'How dare he/she.'

Can you recall anything like that? Yes? No?

Can you begin to see that those thoughts were causing your feelings? If you can't, don't worry. The more you look in this direction, the more you realise it.

Now, think of when the same person didn't irritate you. If not the same person, make it a different person who acted in the same way. In this scenario, they didn't annoy you, and you just dismissed what they were doing/saying because you were in an upbeat mood and didn't want them to ruin it.

What happened there?

The same kind of scenario, but you felt different in each of them. If external situations cause feelings, you would feel the same in both scenarios. No?

That's because thought is the missing link. You thought differently and hence felt differently. It always works from the inside out, and depending on how aware you are (level of consciousness) at that moment will dictate how you feel. Don't worry. I will discuss more about awareness and levels of consciousness later on in the book.

For now, begin to notice where your feelings are coming from. If you disagree with what I have just said, that's good. But stop and ask yourself. This is a book with words on a page. They can't send feelings into your body, so your feelings of disagreement, where is it coming from?

Clue?

Your thoughts!!!

Now that you have an idea about the three principles and what they mean, it's time to move on to suffering. What is it really when we come from the three principles perspective?

Thought Exercise

Let us do a short thought exercise highlighting how thoughts and feelings are intimately linked.

Find a quiet place where you will not be disturbed for 10-15 minutes. Please close your eyes for each part; it helps focus and concentration.

Good feelings

Think of when you felt amazing, maybe on holiday or with dear friends. Focus on all the details of that time. Notice all around you, see all the sights, hear all the sounds, and begin to notice the feelings that arise. Imagine it like you were actually there. What feelings are you feeling? Are you getting a sense of those fantastic feelings?

Bad feelings

Repeat the above exercise, but this time, think of a time you were feeling particularly low or sad. Don't pick anything too tragic or upsetting — just a time when you didn't feel great. Again, imagine it like it is actually happening now. Can you recreate some of those uncomfortable feelings?

The chances are that you managed to make yourself feel good and bad as you carried out each part. If you struggled, don't worry. As with everything, the more you practice, the better you get at it.

The point of the exercise is to highlight how thought creates feelings, not our circumstances. If real-life external events genuinely caused our feelings, then you would not feel anything when doing this exercise.

Keep trying this exercise during the week, and you will begin to notice the connection between thoughts and feelings.

'The way I see it, if you want the rainbow, you gotta put up with the rain.'

Dolly Parton

What Is Suffering?

Definition of suffering:

'The state of undergoing pain, distress, or hardship.'

Suffering is often characterised as physical or mental. In this case, we will be looking at mental suffering, as this is what the book is about. However, it is worth noting that many physical pains can be linked and caused by mental suffering.

In today's modern world, we see suffering, both mental and physical, all over. It's reported on the news daily. Social media is full of people suffering, albeit behind cute dog-eared filters. We hear about the increase in mental illness. This year, 2020, it is estimated that depression will be the second most significant ailment worldwide after heart disease.

The World Health Organization (WHO) estimates that each year, approximately one million people die from suicide, representing a global mortality rate of 16 people per 100,000 or one death every 40 seconds. By 2020, the death rate is predicted to increase to one every 20 seconds.

That, to me, is something to be concerned about. These statistics need to be addressed and changed for the better. Many organisations, charities, and private businesses are driven to change the above numbers when it comes to people suffering.

The definition of suffering is undergoing pain, distress, or hardship, but what does that mean?

Simply put, suffering is an uncomfortable FEELING in the body. Be it depression, anxiety, worry, hurt, anger, or whatever, it all boils down to a feeling in our body that we do not like. Even 'suffering' is an unpleasant feeling. We know we are suffering because we don't feel good, right?

Where does that suffering come from? Is it from external circumstances?

It can certainly look that way. As I write this, we are sitting in the middle of a worldwide pandemic. People are fearful, uncertain, worried, and concerned. It certainly looks like the pandemic is causing these feelings. It certainly feels like these events are triggering our emotions.

But are they?

Let's take a more in-depth look. Remember, I said that our feelings are intimately linked to our thinking from moment to moment. That it only works one way. That said, it's not the events that are causing these feelings; it's the thinking or thoughts we have about the situation that drive the feelings.

If the event were causing our feelings, everyone would feel the same way, and we know that is not true. We see people who are not following the guidelines set out by the government to stay indoors and isolate. They are not wearing masks, and they seem fine and happy. Why?

It is because they are thinking differently or perhaps not even thinking about the pandemic. They probably aren't watching the news like the masses and are not getting freaked out.

We are not feeling stressed, scared, worried, or anxious because of what is happening in the outside world. We feel that way because we are having stressed, scared, worried, anxious, etc. THINKING about what's going on in the outside world, which is causing those very feelings.

So, now let's look at what is behind our suffering.

'Imagination is the beginning of creation.'

George Bernard Shaw

How We Create Our Suffering

Knowing what we know now about thoughts and feelings, I want to suggest that events don't cause us to suffer. We CREATE suffering within us by thinking about the events that occur.

Let us slow down and reflect. Many people can look at the same situation and have different feelings about it. This is due to us thinking differently. We all live in what is known as separate realities. Every person's thinking is unique and, thus, will experience life differently. We all view the world through the lens of our personal thinking. If we truly know and realise this for ourselves, we can respect and recognise that everyone lives in their own version of the world. It's when we think that our way of thinking and being is the right way and then try to impose that on others that leads to conflict. Why?

Because we THINK our personal view is being violated and thus needs defending. It's all made of thought. Everything we experience is made up of the three principles.

We think, and our consciousness brings those thoughts to life via our senses.

Let's backtrack. We are born with complete mental health. You can see this in kids. They are full of joy and happiness. They live in the present moment and experience bliss. When upset, hurt, or hungry, they fully express themselves. Cry or have tantrums, then, when it's over, they return to their well-being and carry on as if nothing happened. They are fully present, living in joy and mental health.

Then, as we grow up, we develop an awareness of ourselves and our thoughts, and based on our experiences, we begin to form a 'personality.' We learn about the law, what the boundaries are, and what is right and wrong. We develop concepts and ideas about the world and about who we are as a person. Many begin to move away (including me) from being present in the moment and experiencing our joy and mental health and start to live in a world of thoughts in our heads. We worry about the past and future and rarely live in the present moment.

We begin to speed up, rushing here, there, and everywhere, both physically and mentally. Our minds start to work overtime, and we continuously live with uncomfortable feelings.

We think the solution to getting rid of these feelings

is to do more and learn more, all in an attempt to find peace of mind and happiness.

Now, we don't do this all the time. We sometimes give ourselves a break and 'chill out' or go on holiday. We feel better, and we attribute those feelings to going on holiday.

Therefore, I must work harder, make more money, and become more successful so I can take more holidays and feel at peace.

We compare our lives to others.

'They have it so much better than I do.'

'They're so lucky.'

We think more, compare more, and feel worse. We drink, smoke, do drugs, have sex, or whatever it is to feel better. Those things begin to be the solution.

Or we go the other way. We begin to isolate ourselves from others and become disconnected and lonely. We could be surrounded by loved ones but cut ourselves off from love.

Our thoughts go on a downward trajectory, driving us into more and more suffering and misery.

Anxiety starts leading to depression and potentially worse. We begin to entertain thoughts that we usually wouldn't, and because we engage them, they persist and become ever more present. This can be the start of suicidal ideation.

Can you see how we do it? How we create our suffering? And can you see how it doesn't come from the outside?

It's an inside job. We create our suffering by our thinking and not only that. We take our thinking seriously.

We believe everything we think, and thus, the feelings worsen. Our suffering and mental illness is an inside job!

Awareness Exercise

The next time you feel down or upset, try to stop and catch what is happening inside your mind.

Notice what thoughts are running through and how you are feeling.

Equally, the next time you feel good, try to catch what thoughts are going through your mind. Is it quieter in your mind when you feel good than when you feel bad?

Can you see a link?

'A belief system is nothing more than a thought you've thought over and over again.'

Wayne W. Dyer

Reconsidering Beliefs

Beliefs are synonymous with the self-help industry.

'You need to change your negative beliefs!'

'Change your limiting beliefs!'

But what are beliefs? The dictionary defines it as:

'The feeling of being certain that something exists or is true.'

I would add that our thoughts create those feelings, and we accept them as gospel. From a young age, we learn and accept who we are by what our parents, teachers, and friends tell us. We usually don't stop to consider the validity of what is being said. If someone who loves and cares for us has said it, it must be true.

We form many 'negative beliefs' about ourselves by what we hear. Then, the fatal mistake is that we accept them to be true. It becomes deeply etched into our 'personality.' We continue our journey through life, adding more and buying into those beliefs about ourselves. Then, at some point, we decide (or get sold on the idea) that we must improve ourselves.

That if you want to:

'Make it,'

'Be happy.'

'Be significant.'

Then, we must 'work' on ourselves to fix all the faults. After all, if we want all the good things in our lives, and we don't have them, then we must not be functioning correctly to attain them. We then begin our never-ending journey down the self-improvement path. Buying books and courses and attending seminars, all with the promise of getting the life we so badly desire.

We innocently accept that we have faulty beliefs that are holding us back. If we can somehow change them, we will be all good. We can then be happy, achieve, and be merry.

Consider this.

What if beliefs are no more than thoughts that we have given too much credit to? We have accepted those negative thoughts to be part of who we are. That we have innocently taken those thoughts as true. I propose that beliefs are no more than thoughts that we hold on to and are no more real than a mirage in the desert. It looks real but vanishes into thin air as you get close. This is the truth of beliefs. They are no more real than a mirage, but we never get up close and watch them vanish.

Let me put it another way. Imagine holding your arm out with a heavy book in your hand. You go through life unable to do everything you want because you're carrying this heavy book out in the air. Your arm hurts and develops all this suffering and restrictions because of it. You think this book is a part of you. You go and see various specialists to help you get rid of the pain and to help you feel free. They do their magic, which helps, but the pain inevitably returns.

Then, one day, you come across someone wise and wonderful (See 'About the Author' at the end of the book – just kidding) who points out that you've been carrying this heavy book around for no reason and can just let it go. This both shocks and surprises you, but you do as suggested. At first, it feels strange and possibly even uncomfortable to let go as you held on for so long. But then, everything starts to feel better, and you no longer have any pain or suffering. It seems so miraculous, and you start looking for other things that you no longer need to hold onto. You unburden yourself of things that no longer serve you by simply letting go. You may, on the odd occasion, pick up a heavy book and begin carrying it around as it was such a habit, but you quickly catch yourself and let go every time.

This is precisely the same as negative beliefs. Once you recognise that, you can let go.

Examine Your Beliefs

Take a pen and paper and write down all your negative beliefs about yourself.

Take your time and compile a good list.

Now, take each belief and really scrutinise it. Is it really true about you?

Are there times when you did things that were contrary to these beliefs?

As you go through each one, ask yourself if it's time to let go of these heavy books and start living a life of freedom.

'Don't count the days; make the days count.'

Muhammed Ali

There Is Only ONE Mental Illness

According to the DSM 5 (The Diagnostic and Statistical Manual of Mental Disorders – 5th Edition), there are a whopping 157 different types of mental illness. That is a shockingly huge number. Some of the most common ones are:

Clinical depression
Bipolar disorder
Psychosis and Schizophrenia
Anxiety disorders

We hear much about the above four in the media and social media, but what is mental illness?

The American Psychiatry Association describes mental illness as:

'Health conditions involving changes in emotion, thinking, or behaviour (or a combination of these). Mental illnesses are associated with distress and/or problems functioning in social, work, or family activities.'

Given the above, what then causes mental illness?

According to WebMD

'Although the exact cause of most mental illnesses is not known, it is becoming clear through research that many of these conditions are caused by a combination of biological, psychological, and environmental factors.'

With so many complex illnesses, treatment can also become long and complicated. Many therapeutic models aim to address the symptoms using medication combined with getting to the cause of suffering by seeing a psychologist or counsellor. Other interventions, such as CBT (Cognitive Behavioural Therapy) a talking therapy, are used to manage your problems by changing how you think and behave. It is most commonly used to treat anxiety and depression but can be helpful for other mental and physical health problems.

These are great interventions, and I have used them myself and with clients. However, they require a lot of work, must be continuously applied to make a difference, and don't always work.

These interventions work to correct something that has already happened. You have negative thinking, and the intervention tries to change or eliminate it. It is an outside-in approach.

As a side note, many people seek therapy because they think something is wrong with them. That somehow, they are broken and need to be 'fixed.' This is and never will be the case. We are always whole and complete. We sit in the middle of perfect mental health but take ourselves away from it using the power of thought. We do this innocently as we don't know any better. No one has told us about the nature of our experience and how our minds work.

All feelings are normal, even the uncomfortable ones. We get ourselves into trouble because we try to escape those feelings. We THINK we shouldn't be feeling them. We aim to be perfect and never have negative thoughts or feelings again. This is a futile attempt because those feelings are inbuilt. They are part of our design. They are there for a reason, and I will get on to what that is later in the book. But, for now, realise and understand the above.

Dr Bill Pettit is a licensed Psychiatrist with over 35 years of experience in the field. He himself suffered from clinical depression until he discovered the three principles and was personally mentored by Sydney Banks for 26 years. This new understanding returned him to his innate health and well-being, and he began sharing it with clients to produce some fantastic results. Since then, more and more psychologists, counsellors, psychiatrists, and mental health professionals have started sharing this understanding with clients and are seeing excellent results regularly. (you can find out more in the resources section at the back of the book.)

While working with patients, he realised that there is only one mental illness. Only one! Sounds crazy, right? I've just said that the DSM 5 has over 157 mental illnesses recorded, but Mr Pettit suggests there is only one!

So, what is the only mental illness? It is,

CHRONIC MENTAL STRESS.

That's right, chronic mental stress is the only mental illness; all the others are different variations of the above.

He truly sees and believes that, but for our thinking, we are all sitting in perfect mental health. Our thinking takes us away from our mental health. He suggests that more severe conditions such as Bipolar disorders, Psychosis, and Schizophrenia are more extreme versions of chronic mental stress.

Remember, I said that our feelings are connected to our thoughts? Dr Pettit talks about feelings being feedback regarding our thinking. The worse we feel indicates that we have too much thinking or thoughts buzzing around in our heads and are engaging too much with them.

Depending on their severity, our feelings tell us that our thinking is off track, that we are going down the wrong path, and that we should stop and relax. But what do we do? We speed up, start thinking, and ponder more. We try to think our way out of the negative feelings, leading to more uncomfortable feelings. The more severe the emotions, the more the system tells you that you are going the wrong way.

The system then makes the signal worse and worse in an attempt to tell you to back off your thinking, but since no one ever told us this, we think more, leading to depression and other conditions as outlined by the DSM 5.

According to Dr Pettit, the more severe conditions are due to chronic mental stress over a more extended and sustained period.

The more we look in this direction, the more it begins to make sense. We feel good when we're not overthinking and are present in the moment. Then, a thought crosses our mind. We start thinking and begin to get uncomfortable feelings (the system tells you that you are engaging with thoughts too much). The more we engage, the worse we feel. The longer this goes on, it will lead to chronic mental stress – the longer it goes on, the more severe the chronic mental stress becomes. It also de-regulates our body chemistry, leading to physical symptoms such as back pain and migraines.

When we look in this direction, it makes sense that we think our way into problems and suffering. The next logical question is, what can we do about it?

Time to Ponder

Start to think and reflect on the mental illness you suffer from (if you do).

Begin to cast doubt on the suffering. See what happens if you start to take your thinking less seriously.

Begin to doubt your doubts.

If we didn't have labels such as 'anxiety' and 'depression,' would they just be uncomfortable feelings, like having a bad day?

Start to question the labels you have for yourself. Do they always hold up as accurate? Or are there days when things are different?

You may find this an interesting and beneficial exercise to do.

'Your thoughts are like the artist's brush. They create a personal picture of the reality you live in.'

Sydney Banks

The Solution

The nature of the principles is that they are a description of how we experience life, not a prescription. If we are not broken or lacking anything, there is nothing to fix. There is nothing to do!

One of the principles is consciousness or awareness. I want to use a metaphor to try to explain this. Imagine one of those lifts made of glass you see on the outside of modern buildings. This lift runs from the bottom of the building in the depths of the basement garage, right the way up to the top. This lift represents our level of consciousness.

The lift naturally sits around two-thirds of the way up the building. Here, we are sitting in a good, healthy state. Our minds are relatively clear, and we have a good view outside the lift. We have a clear perspective and don't take things too personally or seriously. We feel at peace, and life is good. At this level, we are in a good mood and have a high level of consciousness.

Now, as we start to think about things, such as things that happened to us in the past or focusing on things that can go wrong in the future, the lift begins to go down. Our moods begin to drop, and we start to develop uncomfortable feelings such as nervousness or anxiety. We don't like how we feel and begin to think more, trying to think our way out of it. This sends the lift down further. The thinking we do to get out of those uncomfortable feelings is like trying to get the lift to go back up by pressing the down button. The more we get caught up in our thinking, the more we push the down button, and the worse we feel. We try using tools and techniques; sometimes, they work - our thinking settles, and the lift moves up. But more often than not, those tools and techniques require us to engage with our thinking further, and we press the down or hold button, and we either feel worse or remain the same. Our levels of consciousness drop, and we become less aware of us creating our suffering. Our mental health suffers, and our mood drops down further. If we spend more time here, in our heads, thinking and overthinking, we end up suffering from chronic mental stress.

We do this innocently as we don't know any better. The lift drops all the way down to the basement. It's dark and dingy, and from this level of awareness, we think that life happens to us. The world causes us to feel how we feel, which seems real. At this level, we don't recognise, understand, or forget that our feelings come from thought and not outside events. At this level, we take things personally and get offended, upset, and angry. At this level, we feel disconnected from people and spend much time living in our heads. We think about the past or future and are rarely fully present. The longer we stay down here, the worse it can become. We find that the lift can go even deeper and lower into the ground, resulting in more severe mental illnesses. We are pressing the down button in the lift, trying to go up, back to our wellbeing. It doesn't work, so we think the lift is broken. Something is wrong with the lift. It needs fixing.

But the lift is not broken. You just haven't been shown how it works. The designers of the lift were geniuses. They had programmed in a system that if no buttons were pressed, the lift would automatically return up the building and stop about two-thirds of the way up. Back to innate health and well-being.

If someone had told us that if the lift begins to go down (overthinking and feeling bad), not to press any buttons (try your best not to change, engage, etc. with your thinking), the lift will return to its natural resting position.

As you become more aware of how the lift works, you raise your level of consciousness and know that doing nothing when the lift begins to drop is the best way to return to its natural resting position.

Knowing this allows you not to take your thinking too seriously. You don't have to believe everything you think. As your level of consciousness rises, you will find that you spend more time in innate health and less time in mental illness and suffering.

Sound too simplistic?

Well, you're right, it is. It is remarkably simple, but it's not easy. We are humans, and we get caught up. It's natural and ok. You will find that you will catch yourself doing it, remind yourself about your feelings, and then do your best to leave your thinking alone and let your mind settle.

As you see this more deeply, you may find that your lift will rise above the two-thirds mark, and you will begin to find more joy and peace. You will have more beautiful feelings and recognise that this is home — your natural state. You are present. You are fully aware.

You will recognise more and more that your thoughts cause your feelings, and if you start to feel down, upset, etc., then you know your feelings are telling you that the lift is on the way down and you had better stop pushing buttons and let it return to its natural resting place.

Slow Down

The key to really making a difference is slowing down. By this, I mean slowing down in your head.

Most of our suffering occurs when we rev up the mental RPMs (revolutions per minute like the dial in your car).

The RMPs are around the idle mark when we are calm and ok. The mind is relaxed, and thoughts are flowing nicely. We are present and enjoying the moment. It can also be known as 'flow state.'

As we get caught up in our thinking and create our suffering, the RPMs go up and continue to go up as we get more and more caught up. The mind is literally speeding up.

As you recognise this is happening, the trick is to slow down. Take some deep breaths and acknowledge what is happening.

Bring those RPMs down as best you can by slowing down and leaving you thinking alone as best you can.

'Connection is why we are here. We are hardwired to connect with others'

Brene Brown

Connection With Others

If you stop and look at the happiest people around the globe, you will find many things in common, but what I want to talk about here is connection.

They all have a sense of connection with others. They have a group of people who support and care for them. Deeper still, they have a deep-felt sense of appreciation and gratitude for the people they are connected to.

Isolation or the feelings of isolation (coming from thoughts) are leading causes of anxiety and depression. Many people have many connections to many people, but the difference is that they are mostly superficial.

The real sense of connection occurs in the absence of thinking. When we are fully present with others and open our hearts. This is now being called being 'vulnerable.' The new label of the day. To me, it is being human. We open up, connect with others, and feel cared for and supported through highs and lows, through mistakes and successes. This forms bonds of connection with others. This is what we are hardwired to do.

This connection is an integral part of mental health and well-being. When we lose touch with our innate health, love, and connection, our level of consciousness drops, and our thinking spirals out of control. This will always lead to suffering and chronic mental stress.

We begin to think that we are different and don't fit in. That somehow, we cannot connect with people. We become very 'self' orientated and driven, leading to feelings of isolation and loneliness. The spiral continues unless you recognise what is happening. That you are in that lift, pressing down. You realise that you're carrying that heavy book again. Then, all you have to do is stop pressing the button and let go of the book. As you do, you will return to that innate well-being, mental health and clarity.

If we begin to recognise how we create our suffering and misery and how our minds operate, we can start to allow the flow of life to occur. As we do this, we automatically move away from 'self' fixation and loneliness to connection to others, love, and a new appreciation of life.

Social media, like Facebook and Instagram, have brought the world together. We are more digitally connected than ever. However, with all this connectivity, people feel more isolated and alone. Why is that?

My take is that social media has become the theatre of life, where people post polished and beautiful experiences from the sunny shores of paradise, with the hidden commentary suggesting:

'Look how great my life is. Don't you wish you were me or doing as well as me?'

We look at this theatre performance and get sucked right in. Our thoughts begin to spiral out of control, and the feelings of inadequacy and inferiority kick in, all from looking at a bloody post. How messed up is that?

Now, I'm not suggesting for one minute that this is the intention of the people posting the extraordinary life, but it's easy to see how people feel disconnected and upset.

Let's maybe look at social media for what it really is. A stage show, and instead of feeling inadequate, we enjoy and rejoice in the performance. Look upon it as entertainment rather than a personal inventory of how our lives are compared to theirs.

We need to reconnect with each other again, away from social media. In-person, laughing, joking, crying, and sharing woes. This is the root of being human. A sense of community and connection is vital for mental health and well-being.

Building Your Ability to Connect

Start by going for a walk, but this time, instead of being in your head thinking, aim to be present in nature. Take in all the sights and sounds and look for the beauty in nature. Connect with all around you and appreciate the beauty and abundance surrounding you.

You can also do this the next time you're around people. Instead of being in your head, thinking about how to be impressive, aim to be fully present with the people around you. Listen like you want to know, talk less, and listen more.

Let go of the book you carry around when around people, and learn to let your well-being show. Begin connecting.

There is no doubt that you have done this before. It happens all the time when you are out enjoying yourself, being present, and fully connecting. Make a habit of practising it. Don't worry about being perfect or getting it right. Just do; you will slowly connect with others and your innate mental health.

'Seriousness is a disease of the ego.'

Stuart Wilde

You Take Life Too Seriously

Dr Bill Pettit once said that seriousness is the most under-diagnosed mental illness out there. Stop and think about that for a second: seriousness being a mental illness?

What happens when we become serious about life?

Seriousness is a major constrictor of your creative potential.

Seriousness is a significant lowering of your level of consciousness. It gives you tunnel vision and limits your problem-solving abilities.

Imagine a long garden hose pipe with flowing water running through it. The water flows easily and smoothly from one end to the other. This represents you in a calm, clear mind, feeling good and flowing with life. The water resembles your thoughts and creative possibilities, flowing easily and gracefully. Problems do not look so bad, and you know you will find solutions to them.

Now imagine the same garden hose with a kink in the middle. This slows the flow of water (fresh ideas and problem-solving abilities) and may even cut the flow completely. This is what seriousness does to you.

It shuts you off from clarity and fresh new thinking. You feel flat, numb, or down and from there, you try to change the world to make yourself feel better.

Think of times when you were stressed. I can guarantee that you were serious at the time too. We have so much on our plate: work, home life, finances, relationships, and with all that buzzing around in our heads, we feel stressed, worried, anxious, and even depressed.

Then we decide it's time to get SERIOUS about life, and things must change.

'I must take all these things causing me to feel this way seriously if I ever want to feel better!'

Sound familiar?

Let's reiterate that the 'stuff' going on in your life, the work, home life, finances, etc., are not the cause of your stressed and worrisome feelings. It is your thoughts, your thinking, ABOUT the above that are causing you feelings. As you know, your level of consciousness has dropped, and the feeling tells you to chill out and let your mind settle. Your body is signalling you to stop what you're doing and reset.

But what do we do? We become ever more serious about our life circumstances and try and find solutions from this poor state of mind. With a kinked garden hose, we are trying to water the flowers to blossom and find that it doesn't work. With a kinked hose (serious mindset), you cannot water anything (find solutions or any decent ones).

We frequently hear, 'It's time to grow up' and get serious about life.' What that does is the opposite and constricts you into a smaller confined space, and from there, you try and change your life circumstances. It doesn't work or works poorly at best.

Try Playing Instead

Play and a light-hearted lifestyle are vital for mental health and well-being. Having fun and engaging in life is essential for health and longevity.

In his book 'Play: How it Shapes the Brain, opens the and Invigorates the Soul', Stuart Brown, M.D., highlights that play is a fundamental biological drive as integral to our health as sleep or nutrition.

Play is akin to raising our level of consciousness. It gets us present and in the moment, opening the mind to new possibilities and insights (new, fresh thoughts).

Watch kids as they play. They get fully involved, encompassed by the thrill and joy of play. You can see that splattered across their faces — loving life and fully engaged.

Stuart goes on to say that:

'Play – defined as purposeless, all-consuming, restorative activity – is the single most significant factor in determining our success and happiness.'

When in a funk, play. That's my suggestion. It will do more for your mental health than sitting there worrying about the problems you desperately need answers to. The trouble is, we've learned to think of play as a waste of time as there is so much to complete. I propose that to effectively and efficiently deal with these 'problems' and 'things to be done' play is key to resetting your mindset. Thus enabling you to get back to your default setting of clarity and mental health. It's akin to unkinking the garden hose. And from that headspace, you will find fresh ideas and thoughts about tackling them going forward.

We learn best through play. We come up with our best ideas through play. You have undoubtedly heard that most people get their best ideas in the shower. It can be any place, but the point is that when people engage in mundane activities, the mind is usually free to explore. The water is flowing through the hose. Our minds are not usually revved up, and it's ticking along at idle speed, allowing fresh ideas to come through.

This is why seriousness is the biggest hindrance to mental health. Now, I know many of you would argue that serious global issues must be addressed and tackled.

I would agree there are IMPORTANT and SIGNIFICANT challenges around the world that need addressing. However, you address these issues with a free-flowing mind, not a constricted, serious one. No radical solutions will be found to these issues from a SERIOUSNESS standpoint. Important? Yes. Significant? Yes. Necessary? Yes. Serious? No!

Think open, light-heartedness, and free-flowing, rather than kinked, restricted seriousness!

Lighten Up

How seriously do you show up to life?

Can you begin to see the link between seriousness and chronic mental stress?

How much time do you spend playing and enjoying life?

Reflect on times when you engaged in play. Were you happier back then?

Are you too serious now?

If so, lighten up, start to play, and enjoy life (without guilt) and watch how your mental health improves and how much better you feel.

'Even if you're on the right track, you'll get run over if you just sit there.'

Will Rogers

Now I Get It, I Will Never Feel Bad Again!

Umm, I'm afraid not. As I said earlier, this is a description of the human experience and not a prescription. We are still human and will still get caught up in our thinking. We will feel down, upset, angry, etc., but the difference is that we will know where those feelings are coming from. We know that we are feeling our thinking in the moment, and if we remember this, we can pull back, allow our thinking to settle, return to a calm state, and respond from there.

Have you noticed when you are in a low level of consciousness (feelings of anger, judgment, upset) that you are always right, and others are wrong? You can't see the wood from the trees, but you are adamant that your way is the only way. Only when we realise our true nature and recognise that we all live in separate realities can we become more compassionate and tolerant of others.

Our mood plays a key role. Low moods are low levels of consciousness that lead to overthinking and taking our thinking seriously, leading to uncomfortable feelings that we don't like. Small things can annoy and grate on us. We tend to be very 'self' focused and uninterested in others. We get caught up in the drama created by the thoughts in our heads. It happens to all of us.

By contrast, we also have good moods or higher levels of consciousness. We feel great and at peace. Our mind is open and flowing, and we pay little or no attention to our thoughts. We are present in the moment and life. The same things that annoyed us in lower levels of consciousness don't have any effect at this higher level. We dismiss things more quickly, and life looks a lot more pleasant. We feel a sense of connection to others and life.

If we suffer, more often than not, we are usually found in lower levels of consciousness. If we are generally happier, we live in higher levels of consciousness. Everyone fluctuates between levels. Some days are better than others, and we respond depending on our consciousness level at that particular time.

People who suffer from depression and other mental illnesses do so because of their low levels of consciousness. Their feelings are telling them that their thoughts are off track, but because they don't know or aren't aware of the fact that the thoughts they are having are causing their feelings, they innocently engage with them, take them seriously, then further add more thoughts on top of that making them feel even worse. They keep pressing the down button, hoping to rise up!

The good news is that by looking in this direction and understanding everything I have mentioned in this book, you will automatically start raising your levels of consciousness. As you begin to see the truth about the principles and see that your thoughts shape your feelings and, thus, your reality, you can open up to life and let go of suffering-inducing thoughts. You can begin to see that it makes no sense to hold on to thoughts from the past. The past is over; what's happened has happened, and as you make peace with that, you can stop taking your negative thinking so seriously and, as a consequence, raise your level of consciousness.

This understanding allows you the freedom to no longer be an innocent victim of your thoughts and let your innate health shine through.

We will all have our ups and downs, but now you know, just like when you do nothing with your thoughts when you're up, doing nothing with your thoughts when you are down is the key to a healthy mind and well-being.

Time to Reflect

Use this time to start reflecting on moods.

How does the world look when you're in a good mood or at a higher level of consciousness?

Are you more tolerant and forgiving?

Are you more accepting?

Do you let things go easier? Do you think about others more?

Now, do the same and reflect on low moods. How much smaller does your world become? In this state, is it all about you and your opinion? Do you find people irritating?

Chances are you are starting to see the role of moods and taking thoughts too seriously. The lower our levels of consciousness, the more seriously we take our thoughts. It's the way we operate. There's nothing wrong with you. It's called being human. Now that you are aware, you have more freedom around how you react to the world.

'Reality is merely an illusion, albeit a very persistent one.'

Albert Einstein

It's All An Illusion

It's all made up. We live in a CONSTRUCT of reality based on our thinking and level of consciousness moment by moment.

None of it is real. It seems very real to us as we are the ones who are creating the experience. It's akin to going to the cinema to watch your favourite film that's been made in 3D with all the latest special effects technology.

You take your seat and get fully absorbed in the movie. You feel the characters' emotions, the highs and lows, and get entirely carried away. You get sucked into the film and experience it like you were there.

The movie ends, and you walk out, thinking it was fantastic, yet you know it wasn't real. It was made up, yet it felt real at the time. This is how your mind works.

It is continually making up what you experience via the three principles, and your consciousness (the special effects department of the mind) makes it appear real. If you don't know this is how the mind works, you believe everything you see and think. Yet it's an illusion of the mind. However, our mind is doing this all the time, 24/7. We live in our own movie.

As we begin to recognise that, we can see the illusion for what it is and not take the movie too seriously, yet it is the best system ever developed, and we will get sucked into it. That's part of being human.

The more we look in the direction of this understanding, the more we begin to get a sense of freedom from the illusion and settle into our innate mental health and well-being more of the time.

We don't escape the human experience, but we can recognise it for what it is — a grand illusion.

That is what the three principles do for us.

The Illusion of Control

We have this notion that we are in control of our lives and what happens to us.

How true is this?

Look how the pandemic has affected millions who assumed they were in control of their lives.

Stop and reflect on how much or little control we actually have.

The traffic, people's behaviour and attitude towards us, the weather, our jobs, family, and children. They are all ultimately out of our control.

The only thing we can really control is our response to what life throws at us. We can get upset and angry at the unfairness of it all, or we can look for the opportunities that life gifts us.

We hear every cloud has a silver lining, so what is the silver lining in your life? How can you look at life differently to make it better?

'Life is an illusionary, spiritual journey, confined within the boundaries of time, space and matter.'

Sydney Banks

What Mental Health Professionals Say

As I said at the beginning of this book, I don't want you to take my word for what I say. I want you to look for yourself and see if it is true for you.

It's easy for me to sit here and say all this, but since I lack any of the recognised official qualifications in mental health, why should you believe me anyway?

Therefore, in this section, I want to mention some of the qualified psychologists, psychiatrists, and counsellors who have all started sharing this understanding with their clients to produce what appears to be miraculous results.

Below is a list of various mental health therapists who share the principles with their clients or patients. You will find links to their websites in the resources section of this book.

Dr Bill Pettit – Licenced Psychiatrist
Dr Linda Pettit – Licenced Psychologist
Dr Amy Johnson – Social Psychologist
Dicken Bettinger – Clinical Psychologist
Cathy Casey – M.A in Clinical Psychology
Dr Mark Howard – Licenced Psychologist
Dr Joe Bailey – Licenced Psychologist

Dr Suraj Gogoi – Medical Doctor/Psychiatrist
Dr Rani Bora – Medical Doctor/Psychiatrist
Dr Keith Blevens – Clinical Psychologist
Dr Ken Manning – Clinical Psychologist

More and more mental health professionals are looking in the direction of the principles to help themselves, as well as their clients.

They have found that the principles have helped their clients and themselves experience true mental health and understand how we create our suffering.

You can find countless testimonials online to see how this truly impacts people's lives.

'If the only thing people learned was not to be afraid of their experience, that alone would change the world.'

Sydney Banks

Summing It All Up

So here we are, towards the end of the book, and I hope you can see the nature of how your mind works and that there is nothing to fix. You are not broken.

Remember, we live in a world constructed by thought made to appear real by our consciousness. Our thoughts create every feeling we feel, not the events of the outside world.

We always work from the inside – out. But for our thinking, we always sit in the middle of perfect mental health.

Let the above sink in. We are always sitting in mental health. We think and think ourselves away from it.

Slowing down is critical. Slow down and enjoy life. You don't need to be in a rush. The more we slow down, the more the mind settles and the more we see. We get insights into the nature of our experience and suffering.

Mind, thought, and consciousness are the three principles and are always in action from the moment we are born to the moment we die.

Look for yourself into the principles and this understanding. If you look with an open mind, I bet you will see something for yourself.

Remember, you are perfection in action. You've just lost sight of that!

I hope this book has helped you see how we all create our suffering and that from here on in, you will find, recognise, and know that you are sitting in perfect mental health!

What Have You Learnt?

You made it to the end of the book. Congratulations!

What have you learned about how your mind works?

Can you see how you create your suffering?

Do you understand how your state of mind (level of consciousness) is crucial in how you experience life?

Can you see the link between thoughts and feelings?

Can you see that no one can make you feel anything without first thinking about it?

Can you see how to return to your innate mental health and well-being?

I hope you can see all the above and start living light-heartedly and joyfully. Slow down, let your mind settle, and nestle up close with your God-given right to mental health and well-being.

'The soul is your innermost being. The presence that you are beyond form. The consciousness that you are beyond form, that is the soul. That is who you are in essence.'

Eckhart Tolle

BONUS SECTION

**My thoughts on our spiritual
nature, life, and humanity**

WARNING!!!

The book takes on a more spiritual direction from here.

Feel free to miss this part for those with no such interest.

You are free to jump to the resources section and continue your journey of exploring the three principles.

For those who are curious, please continue.

Who Are We Really?

There is a famous saying by Pierre Teilhard de Chardin:

'We are not human beings having a spiritual experience; we are spiritual beings having a human experience.'

Have you stopped to wonder about this?

That we are much more than the physical body we occupy.

We are universal consciousness taking shape in the physical form.

There is a space within which is pure consciousness, pure awareness, and it is within this space that all thoughts come and go.

That space within us contains all the answers you seek for your problems. We tend to look in the wrong direction for problem-solving. I don't mean the typical day-to-day issues. I mean the big ones that fill us with fear or worry.

If you quiet your mind and let go of trying to figure out the problem with your intellect, your inner wisdom will offer solutions that would never have occurred to you otherwise.

That wisdom is you. The infinite creative potential, pure consciousness, is your true self.

Pause and Reflect

This idea can be challenging to get your head around, so take a break here.

Don't think about this too much and in great detail. Trust me, that is a great way to get a headache.

Explore this notion in bite-size chunks. Take your time and enjoy the exploration.

'When you let go of the egoic self, what you're getting in exchange is the whole universe.'

Adyashanti

The Egoic Self

We learn to identify with 'self.' We develop a personality and a sense of 'I.' We separate ourselves from others and confine ourselves into a box with labels attached. We build an identity, values, and beliefs and construct a 'self.' We move away from the spiritual essence and more towards the physical.

We move away from what is invisible and trust that what we see, hear and feel is gospel.

Our ego is always seeing. It looks for what fits into our idea of self and dismisses anything that contradicts or undermines it.

It is the source of all separation and suffering. It lives through comparison, and in this day and age, the ego reigns supreme.

'The ego, however, is not who you really are. The ego is your self-image; it is your social mask; it is the role you are playing. Your social mask thrives on approval. It wants control, and is sustained by power, because it lives in fear'.

Deepak Chopra

Take a look at society today. The mainstream media, advertisers, and social media are all aimed at the ego, feeding it, making us compete against each other, and creating an ever-increasing separation.

Think back to earlier in the book when I talked about isolation and lack of connection. The egoic self is the cause of this suffering. You can think of it as a lower level of consciousness.

As our level of consciousness drops, we drop deeper into the egoic self.

Time to Reflect

In your encounters with people, can you detect a subtle hint of superiority or inferiority towards them?

If so, then that is your ego.

Where else does your ego show up?

I guess that it is prevalent in most areas of your life.

Ask yourself why you think that is.

Why is the ego, the ruler, supreme?

If we recognise that it is the root of all suffering and pain, why are we still living from the ego?

Hint? Look at what information is bombarding you daily. Does it lead to separation and competition?

Our True Nature

As we rise out of the depths of low-level consciousness, we can begin to connect to our true nature. As our awareness increases, we start to see that we are more than our physical bodies.

We are pure awareness having a human experience. If you look, you can notice the space in between your thoughts.

The silence between the noise.

That is your true nature. We are the space from which thoughts arise and pass.

We are the void from which all arises. Thoughts are the vehicle that passes through our awareness to give us the human experience.

We are the absence of ego and the identity of self. We find that empty space that occupies the entire universe, that comprises every living thing on this planet.

It is from this space, within us, that all creativity and innovation come from. It's the space we access when our minds are clear and the noise and RPMs in our minds settle.

This is also known as a flow state. In sports, it is often referred to as the 'zone'.

This state of mind is vital for success in every area of life, from relationships to business success, yet it is so overlooked.

Here is where our levels of awareness rises.

It's when we feel most connected.

It's when we feel the most alive.

It's when we are flowing with unconditional love.

If you stop listening to the marching band continuously playing in your head and instead focus on the silence between the noise, you will discover the wisdom within.

You will discover the real you, the true self, and when you do, you will quickly see there isn't a 'self' at all.

'Our separation of each another is an optical illusion of consciousness.'

Albert Einstein

No 'I,' No 'You,' No Separation

As we become more aware of who or what we really are, we can begin to see that we are all made of the same stuff.

We all come from the same place. We are all pure consciousness. We are all made of energy.

When you recognise that, you start to see that there is no separation. We are all the same. We originate from the same source.

While we all look, think, and act differently, the stuff we are made of is identical.

When we return to the source, there is no 'self'; there is no 'you'. There is no separation.

We begin to see differences as we drop into our human experience and that of the ego. We identify with the self, and the ego starts its journey of creating self-significance.

It is this egoic self that sees separation. It is what creates suffering, pain, and anger.

Moving away from the spiritual towards the physical is the beginning of conflict.

'If you're invested in security and certainty, you're on the wrong planet.'

Pema Chodron

You're Not As Feeble As You Have Been Led To Believe

Your mind, body, and soul have the inbuilt capacity to heal and regenerate.

We are stronger than we know. Resilience is built into the system. The body is fantastic at healing and fighting disease and illness.

The mind has the capacity for infinite possibilities. We can tap into a bottomless well of creativity and weave together ingenious solutions to problems.

Our souls can penetrate the darkest of realms and fill them with light. We can connect, love, sympathise and soothe other souls.

Our ability to be fully responsible for our health and well-being is totally within our control.

Why is it, then, that so many people are struggling?

Why are people suffering mentally, physically, and spiritually?

In my opinion, we are never taught that we are powerful. We are taught dependence. In particular, reliance on the system.

Our educational system teaches us to be useful members of society and hard workers. Don't question the status quo.

Our health care is built around curing illness rather than promoting health. Our minds are repeatedly driven towards negativity. I was never told to look at the silver lining rather than the dark clouds.

All over social media, mental illness is abundant. We have mental health awareness campaigns to make us all aware of the diseases out there.

If this is all we see all over the media, then this is all we see in the 'real world.'

I find it ironic that mental health never talks about mental health. It's loaded with mental illness discussions around stress, anxiety, depression, etc. No amount of talking about mental illness will result in mental health.

We must teach and discuss mental health if we want mentally healthy people. We must educate people not to be afraid of their experiences. To not be scared of their thoughts, to take them less seriously.

Teach people about clarity of mind and the space of wisdom within.

Teach the young that they are perfect as they are. Let people know that they have health and well-being inside of them.

We must nourish the soul and have conversations that include spirituality.

We must show people that we are not separate but part of a greater whole.

We are not weak and feeble beings who need dependency on medication and state funds to survive.

We are the infinite universe within which miracles lay.

The more we have these conversations, the more we can move people away from the egoic self to the true self.

This is how we will have more peace, harmony, and abundance around the globe.

'As you dissolve into love, your ego fades. You're not thinking about loving; you're just being love, radiating like the sun.'

Ram Dass

Pure Awareness and Unconditional Love

The Beetles were on the right track when they sang,

'All you need is love.'

I would take it further and say that you ARE love. Unconditional love. This is what we are at a higher level of consciousness.

As we raise our awareness of our true nature and thus our level of consciousness, we begin to dissolve the ego and the illusion of separation. We fall back into our default setting of love and compassion.

Not romantic love, not love with attachment and conditions. Real unconditional love. Love without attachment.

Loving all that is and ever will be. Loving the world we find ourselves in. We radiate love, and the world begins to change from this perspective.

Coming from a place of love and understanding opens a world of possibilities and solutions. Compare that to the current state of affairs — hatred, anger, and separation from the egoic self.

Ask yourself, honestly, will this ever provide a solution?

Think About It

From which point of view do you believe will produce the most significant change for humanity

Love and understanding?

Or

The egoic self?

Which point of view will bring people together, and which will divide us further?

Which perspective do you usually come from in your own life?

'Bring acceptance into your nonacceptance. Bring surrender into your nonsurrender. Then see what happens.'

Eckhart Tolle

Acceptance And Surrender

What does it mean to accept?

I mean to accept how life is now, in this moment, and to surrender to it. Not the story you create in this moment but the actual moment in its entirety.

We have to embrace what is. Being present and in the flow of life, whatever it brings.

Accept the pain, judgment, and criticism. The ego cannot handle that, but that is not you. That is the human experience you encounter.

As you learn to accept and surrender, much of the event's energy and potency dissipate. With increasing ease and grace, you can flow from one life event to the next.

As simple as it sounds, this is no easy feat. It requires daily work and lifelong practice, but it does start with a decision to flow with life, to accept and surrender. From there, you work daily to allow life to flow and go along for the ride. The highs, the lows, and the plateaus, you accept and surrender to it all.

You say yes to life. Even when your ego is saying no, this will weaken the egoic self and strengthen your connection to your innate wisdom.

Think about what our biggest challenge is in life. It is our illusion that we have control of the direction it takes, then we argue, cry and scream when it veers off course.

We enjoy it when things go our way and detest it when it doesn't.

The real freedom we all seek comes when we surrender to life's course and actions. When we finally realise that we have very little control.

We can sit back and go along for the ride. We will still get caught up in our personal thinking and still cry and moan, but we will then have the choice to accept, let go, surrender and move forward from that state of awareness.

As we become more and more accustomed to living this way, we will find that freedom we seek and know that life always has our back. Even when life throws a bucket of s**t in your direction, it could make fertile ground for something extraordinary to grow.

Accept and Surrender

Try this for a month. See what happens.

For the next month (or week if a month seems too long), say yes to what comes up. Don't fight, argue, or moan, even if you don't like or want to.

Accept what life throws at you and surrender to its will.

Notice how you feel at the end of the month.

Do you have a slight increase in the sense of freedom?

'In the end, only three things matter: how much you loved, how gently you lived, and how gracefully you let go of things not meant for you.'

Buddha

Closing Thoughts

Simplicity is the key component to a happy, fulfilling life.

Living from the ego has become a way of life. Narrowing our awareness and taking our thoughts too seriously is causing us to suffer needlessly.

When we open up to life, accept and surrender, we open up to our inner wisdom. We begin living from our hearts and raising our levels of consciousness. We open up to unconditional love and understanding.

We become more connected to others in ways that seem impossible. We open up to the infinite well of possibility and creativity.

Learn to let go.

Will it matter in the end?

We suffer because we identify with our egoic self. The self that likes to judge, criticise and compare.

What we are is pure consciousness, having an experience of being human and all that it entails.

I know we needlessly create our suffering, but suffering is part of being human. It is not something to be afraid of. If we accept this idea sincerely, we can learn not to fear suffering. It is through suffering that we strengthen and grow.

It becomes a problem when we believe that we shouldn't suffer. That it is somehow unhuman-like. All emotions are natural and to be experienced fully.

Being human is a tiny part of our journey. While we occupy this space and have this human experience, it makes sense to live it fully. To experience it all and to continue to move forward and grow.

Facing our challenges, feeling the fear and doing it anyway. Knowing that in the end, all will be ok.

Be kind, loving and understanding. We are all one. You are a droplet in a vast ocean of droplets. We think we are separate but all made of the same stuff. You are the droplet and the ocean.

We need to stop believing everything we see and hear on the television and the internet. Remember, it has become a grand stage show with a never-ending performance with the intention of sucking you in.

Rile up your ego and create the illusion of separation, difference and lack.

You are whole and complete. Look within yourself. Take time to quiet the mind. Listen for the silence in all the noise. That is where you reside. That is home, and you can return to it at any time.

Recognise that you will go through various emotions on your life's path. Be ok with that. Don't fight what is. Allow, accept, and let it pass. It always does if we allow it. Fighting it keeps it hanging around.

Look for beauty in the world and feel beautiful feelings. Love unconditionally, laugh uncontrollably and cry forcefully.

Experience life in its entirety. Don't get hung up on fixing the world. Be the mirror you want the world to reflect.

If you want peace in the world, find peace in yourself.

If you want mental illness to be a thing of the past, find your mental health and teach people that.

People too often try to fix the world to make themselves feel better, and it's a poor strategy to follow.

Instead, be the change you wish to see. Don't push people to change; that causes rejection and resentment. Anything forced is met with force, either directly or indirectly.

Take people by the hand and guide them; it's a nicer way to create a movement.

You don't have any mental illness. You lose sight of your mental health. You start looking in the wrong direction. All you need do is turn around and head back home to the inner peace that resides in you and everyone.

Don't take the words in this book too seriously. Don't use your intellect to analyse what is being said. Look at what the words are pointing to. It's like Bruce Lee said:

'Don't think, feel...it's like a finger pointing a way to the moon. Don't concentrate on the finger, or you will miss all that heavenly glory.'

Please view this book in the same way. Look at what the words are pointing to. Don't think or overanalyse. This is a felt experience. One which you will experience more and more of as you allow your personal thinking and egoic self to drop away.

You are greater than you know, more powerful than you are aware, and can bounce back from any adversity if you learn not to be afraid of your experience.

As far as I know, we have one life to live. It is a gift from God, and I would hate to think we would waste it by living fearfully.

Be at peace with all that you are, flaws and all.

Live with a lightness in your heart and a spring in your step.

Live like you had no thoughts at all.

Resources

Websites:

www.thedrspettit.com
This is Dr Bill Pettit and Dr Linda Pettit's website. Here you can find information about them and their work.

www.dramyjohnson.com
This is Dr Amy Johnson's website. Here is a ton of information about the principles. She has a great blog and podcast worth listening to.

www.3principlesmentoring.com
This is Dicken Bettinger's website, where you can learn about him and his work.

www.threeprinciplesinstitute.org
Dr Mark Howard's website about the principles and his work.

www.joebaileyandassociates.com
Dr Joe Bailey's Website. Lots of information, including videos and blogs.

www.Drsranisuraj.com
Dr Rani Bora and Dr Suraj Gogoi's website.

www.threeprinciplesparadigm.com
Dr Keith Blevens and Valda Monroe's website. A lot of information and some great products.

www.alittlepeaceofmind.co.uk
Nicola Bird's website. Loads of information, products, coaching, blog, and podcast.

www.michaelneill.org
This is Michael Neill's website. He is one of my favourite speakers in the three principles world— lots of information on the website with articles, products, and podcast.

www.3pgc.org
This is the three principles global community website. Here, you will find loads of resources all about the three principles, as well as finding practitioners.

www.beyond-recovery.co.uk
This is Jacqueline Hollow's website. She works with young people with drug and alcohol issues in the community and prisons.

www.sydbanks.com
A website dedicated to Sydney Banks. You can watch some of his lectures and listen to his audios here.

Books:

All books by Sydney Banks:

The Missing Link
The Enlightened Gardener
Dear Liza
Second Chance
In Quest of The Pearl

The Inside-Out Revolution, Michael Neill

The Space Within, Michael Neill

Coming Home: Uncovering the Foundations of Psychological Well-being, Dicken Bettinger, Natasha Swerdloff

Victim of Thought: Seeing Through the Illusion of Anxiety, Jill Whalen

Little Peace of Mind: The Revolutionary Solution for Freedom from Anxiety, Panic Attacks and Stress, Nicola Bird

Living Fearlessly, Rachel Henke

I Am Just A Woman: My story of domestic violence, recovery from PTSD & waking up to a whole new life, Mary Schiller.

Somebody Should Have Told Us! (Simple Truths for Living Well), Jack Pransky

One Thought Changes Everything, Mara Gleason

The Relationship Handbook: A simple guide to satisfying relationships, George S. Pransky

Island of Knowledge, Linda Quiring

Beyond Beliefs: The Lost Teachings of Sydney Banks, Linda Quiring

Nuggets of Wisdom: Learning to see them, Elsie Spittle

How to Turn Stress on Its Head: The simple truth that can change your relationship with work, Dr Rani Bora

About The Author

Ravinder Gino Hoonjan is the owner and director of Bright Mind Consulting. A qualified mindset coach and sports massage therapist. His journey in personal development spans over 25 years. Gino suffered from a severe lack of confidence, self-esteem, and low self-worth during childhood. Due to this, the pursuit and interest in personal development took off. Gino became fascinated with how the human mind works and how we can make our minds work for us rather than against us. This led him to become a hypnotherapist, Master NLP practitioner, CBT practitioner, Hypno-coach, and a member of the prestigious 'Hypnotherapy Society'. Since then, He has been helping people become the best version of themselves physically, mentally and emotionally.

As well as working with hundreds of clients on a 1-2-1 basis, which include:

- Burnout executives - Coaching to transform their state of mind to that of high performance without burnout
- Sales professionals - To improve sales numbers by eliminating negative self-talk, fear of rejection
- Business Owners - To improve sales by highlighting blind spots

- MMA fighters - Mindset and flow state training (also known as the 'zone') for peak performance
- Professional Cricketers - Mindset and flow state training for peak performance
- Strongman athletes - Mindset and flow state training for peak performance

He has worked with many large organisations, including

- Rackspace
- American Airlines
- DHL

His work with organisations is heavily focused on the employee, educating them on the workings of the mind and how we create our reality. The implications of this profound understanding result in

- Dramatic decrease in stress and anxiety
- Increase in productivity
- Increase in team synergy and cohesion
- Increase in creativity and problem-solving
- Increase in bottom-line figures

During the Covid lockdown, Gino wrote his book, 'How We Create Our Suffering And What We Can Do About It'. This short book was written to help people understand their minds, how we create our own problems, and what we can do about it.

Post-COVID, he recognised a sharp decline in mental health for many people, which led him to create his popular product,

'The Fearless Life' Card Deck (https://personalprogress.co.uk/fearless).

A neat little product that helps people with simple reminders and tasks that help improve mental health and state of mind.

Should you or your organisation want to know more, you can contact Gino at

gino@brightminds.global

Or you can visit

www.BrightMinds.global

Printed in Great Britain
by Amazon

28478484R00079